Self - confidence, Self - esteem for happiness and success.

Love, respect and honor yourself.

Gautam Sharma

This book is dedicated to my valued readers

Copyright

TABLE OF CONTENTS

Introduction

a) For the Lord will be your confidence and keep you safe always (the Scriptures)

b). Follow the path of karma and you will find all confidence and value within yourself (the Vedas).

From as early as the Scriptures and the Vedas until recent scientific research, studies and writings confirm that with self-belief and confidence we can be healthy, happy and successful. You can make it a habit to use self-confidence and self-belief to put aside problems and start living fuller lives. Those who feel that life is difficult and that everybody must fight for everything in life will find the contents of this book beneficial for self-improvement This book is based on extensive research and analytical findings. Over time it has been conclusively proven that our attitude determines the outcomes of our efforts and hence brings about good or bad experiences.

CHAPTER ONE

Do you sometimes wish what you could make your life experiences consistently joyous and successful? Do you feel worthy and deserving enough to be a lovable person having and enjoying a healthy and a fulfilled lifestyle? Would you like to boost your self-worth and your true value to their ultimate levels? Several types of people read this book: first those with healthy self-worth, some others with low self-worth and the third kind being those with over-inflated self-worth. Individuals with low and highly inflated self-worth are both unhappy and dissatisfied; they are just different sides of the same bad coin (insecure and unbalanced). Low self-worth often results in not bringing to fruition what people desire. On the other hand, extreme, over inflated self-worth shows results faster and seemingly easily but largely with restrictions , mostly attracting people/things which are meaningless and misplaced and which cannot be enjoyed (cases as: a mansion but not a home, or being in a marriage but without mutual love and respect, or an apparently high-profile job that materializes but turns into something unnerving and disappointing and furthermore doesn't last long).Although self-worth and self-esteem are a bit interrelated, they both have different implications. Health and personality research studies link self-esteem with confidence (people's abilities to accomplish things, their general motivation and energy resources). For specific tasks such people are accomplished, take smart decisions, are capable and hard working-they have self-esteem in their work. they are also confident with their educational background, their sociability and ability to lead, therefore they have high self-esteem about how they work and communicate. Different from this, self-worth is the self-assessment of our comprehensive value (to what extent we deserve goodness in our lives, the quantity and kinds of things/accomplishments, that we deserve, that we have good qualities and we have achieved good things).However, achievements are reflected in different ways : one way is material things(a compatible companion, a large house, elegant diamond jewelry, fancy new car, or other upscale possessions) ;other achievements are in terms of intangibles (leadership, fame, authority, respect, status, friendship and love).In order to estimate your own esteem, without over or under rating yourselves, start with analyzing what you find worthwhile. Reflecting on what really matters to you, deciding about these to fit into your lifestyle (what is important and worthwhile), such an analysis may take a long time. The complete process is complex and can stretch over years the process can also get bogged down with events that cause us uneasiness and playout things we don't want or don't cherish. Once done correctly, we can come up with our priorities which can serve as our personal positioning system(PPS) for where we are and where we want to go.

CHAPTER TWO

Given here is an evaluation format which you may find useful to measure your self-worth and how to improve it. This is given in systemic stages to help you connect with your own self-worth. Many have found this useful and benefited from it. Let's use this practical, stage-wise format to measure self-worth and create a stronger and healthier foundation:

Stage One) Think about what you admire in other people. For instance, you may admire people who show confidence, make friends easily, who are outgoing, good at conversation, influence others with their lifestyle (sociable, well-placed extroverts). You admire many other qualities, but to keep the evaluation concise, let's keep it to just one set of qualities. Keep in mind that this is personality analysis, so qualities you admire will be totally unique for you, it's not whether it's is good or bad to judge by moral standards Also, what we admire now will evolve over time (these qualities will be different 10 years from now) and will need re-evaluation after a decade.

Stage Two) Review what you wrote in Stage One and ask yourself: are some of these qualities in you too?

Stage Three) Mentally reaffirm that the qualities you admire in others, yet you find missing in yourself are areas of personal growth that will help you to strengthen yourself-worth. Once you define some things you admire in other people, check again to see if, at least, you have similar strengths. All that you lack are noticeable areas of personal growth for your healthier, happier self-worth.

Stage Four) With some quiet thinking, check within yourself what actions you need to take to build up qualities you admire but don't possess (by using a positive outlook and without feeling inadequate, at any stage) and then start taking corrective steps daily towards your desired goals. Depending on how low the individual self-worth level was set at, it will need that much correcting to boost it. Self-worth qualities are building blocks which can be assembled with the foundation first and upwards to make a strong structure of strengths. It needn't be toiling work or a chore to finish. We can make self-worth improvement as an ongoing, fun-filled and enjoyable process while celebrating each milestone and subtle growth and development. Surveys show that developing new, valuable qualities within ourselves pays off large dividends by lifting our self-worth levels up to their ultimate levels and feeling wonderful about ourselves now and for good.

Stage Five). Realize that worthwhile goals may take time and consistent effort to reach and to perfect; the process is essentially redefining oneself and keep reforming and evolving. Following the above example, if you admire confident, outgoing people but you are presently shy and an introvert, then start taking daily steps to boldly face your doubts and fears, clean up your negative patterns, join public speaking classes, take help by learning from your outgoing relatives/friends, even fail a few times in meeting new people but be persistent, get up, dust yourself off and keep on going. Once you have reset your consciousness onto a higher level of boldness and confidence and you visualize yourself as confident and bold already, you will get more insights into how to achieve improved personality and habits. You have now set goals on what you admire, you visualize yourself getting to be good at those traits, follow the solutions that come to you and stay the course. You will get there and feel joyous and wonderful with your newly found strong and healthy self-esteem

esteem. Stage Six) Clearly visualize your new personality and how you would be behaving with confidence and your strong belief in yourself. Knowing you're worthy and acting like you are valuable are different. Quite often, we understand the rationale for things but are not able to internalize it. However, by consistently synchronizing thoughts with actions we can achieve set goals.

Stages even) Make these a habit in your daily life. Once you have focused on and followed up on the above-mentioned stages, you will feel and appreciate a boost in your self-esteem and self-confidence. Keep focused on the positive, because whatever you focus on expands So expand on the positives of who you are and all that you have. Give thanks and be grateful for the fact that you are alive, be thankful that you have enough air to breathe and since you can breathe, you can smell the freshness of nature and the roses. Be thankful for the fact that the sun, air and water keep all humans, other live forms and vegetation alive. We all have so many things to be grateful about. the list would run into dozens or even hundreds and thousands. With the habit giving thanks and being grateful, you are increasing the flow of goodness that you receive. A very simple yet effective affirmation to repeat in your mind is: "I deserve the best, expect the best and receive the best right now and at all times". Say the above and believe that soul is all right and doing all right regardless of what is going on. Have ongoing faith in the Universe and you will receive abundance of goodness. There is so much abundance of what Divinity has granted you and the more you dwell on abundance and the goodness, the more you will receive." Conceive, believe and achieve" is not a mere slogan, it is the foundation for manifesting positive energy vibrations in the form of material things Divinity has shaped this law for all living beings from the dawn of creation forever. Thought process is essential for creating our constantly evolving lives. Your thoughts completely give shape to our experiences and to material things in your lives.

Our lives are how we shape them with our thoughts. From the varied background of our thoughts and belief systems, we create everything in the way of who we are and all that we have. Thousands a bit fascinating and somewhat magical, doesn't it? But that's how it works; just by thinking of positive outcomes most of the times, we get them to manifest for us. It is logical that to direct our life outcomes, we must learn to control the nature of our recurring and dominant mental self-talk. Peaceful, harmonious, loving self-talk is achievable with a fair amount of focus and regular practice that we can continue to draw only positive experiences in your life.

CHAPTER THREE

A. Trust the Universe: You are part of Divine creation and a magnificent expression of life. Embrace and accept your oneness with Divinity and repeat this in your thoughts and in words upon awakening, during the day and just before going to sleep:" I am one with Divinity and a magnificent expression of divine life. I am meant to be safe, secure and well in all possible ways at all times."

B. Keep focused on the positive, because whatever you focus on expands So expand on the positives of who you are and all that you have. Give thanks and be grateful for the fact that you are alive, be thankful that you have enough air to breathe and since you can breathe, you can smell the freshness of nature and the roses. Be thankful for the fact that the sun, air and water keep all humans, other live forms and vegetation alive. We all have so many things to be grateful about. the list would run into dozens or even hundreds and thousands. With a habit giving thanks and being grateful, you are increasing the flow of goodness that you receive. A very simple yet effective affirmation to repeat in your mind is: "I deserve the best, expect the best and receive the best right now and at all times". Say the above and believe that you are all right and doing all right regardless of what is going on. Have ongoing faith in the Universe and you will be doing all right

There is so much abundance of what the Creator has granted you and the more you dwell on abundance and the goodness, the more you will receive." Conceive, believe and achieve" is not a mere slogan, it is the foundation for manifesting positive energy vibrations in the form of material things Divinity has shaped this law for all living beings from the dawn of creation forever.

Thought process is essential for creating our constantly evolving lives. Your thoughts completely give shape to our experiences and to material things in your lives.

Our lives are how we shape them with our thoughts. From the varied background of our thoughts and belief systems, we create everything in the way of who we are and all that we have. Sounds a bit fascinating and somewhat magical does [t it? But that's how it works; just by thinking of positive outcomes most of the times, we get them to manifest for us. It is logical that to direct our life outcomes, we must learn to control the nature of our recurring and dominant mental self-talk. Peaceful, harmonious, loving self-talk is achievable with a fair amount of focus and regular practice that we can continue to draw only positive events into our lives; all what we intend to have and experience for better living. The power of positive thinking can help you achieve everything, once you accept the truth that your thoughts create your reality. - right now, and into the future. In very practical ways and encouraging terms, we are entirely the true creators of our own world, every time and under all circumstances We ourselves shape our lives with our thoughts, words, beliefs and feelings. At first glance this logic may perhaps seem false, irrelevant or baseless because some can instantly point to events that were seemingly beyond your control: your birth circumstances, some illnesses, some accidents, your enemies, and that storm or hurricane that killed so many. Because no one says to themselves: it's okay that I sometimes get harmed, mugged or cheated."

So, let's get to the core of the universal truth with precision.: at mostly subconscious levels—starting long before birth and then with cumulative beliefs that were once subconscious¬ —you created them all: every event, detail and therefore all happenings in your lives.

Before birth we have chosen the pathways; during life we choose the lanes. One perfectly functional, healthy body, millions of arteries

To sum up, your mental patterns are truly your fixed life: genetics, ancestry, continent skin form, body shape and so like on as well as some predefined milestones like specific family members, a serious setback, a windfall inheritance or newly found fortunes. You then choose your arterial pathways every second of your waking lives—with your thinking. Simply put, your thoughts accumulate and become potent beliefs, the strongest ones operating at subconscious levels and affecting your next sequence in life choices. Little wonder that when something unpleasant happens, we think that we got a bad deal.

Respond to the call to action, move away from mere existence towards joyous living.

Start believing that everyone is part of Divinity and truly magnificent., You are one with the ultimate source-the Super consciousness". These are proven values in spirituality for over 3,000 years and will continue remain valid to uplift humanity.

The truth above compliments the laws of contemporary science and metaphysics. Modern scientists, researching about the fundamental building blocks of the universe are discovering other laws. Here's one: both the presence and the behavior of subatomic particles depend on what is going on in the mind of the scientist".

"This may sound a bit fictional make believe but is really scientifically true and has been replicated many times. The implications are stunning. As one expert science researcher put it, "Physicists these days are uncovering untapped frontiers."

Conventional science assumes that consciousness arises from physical objects. Metaphysics states that the reverse is true too, something which Asian Hindu Masters have known for 3,000 years. No wonder that Buddha (the enlightened) put it this way: "All that we are is the result of what we have thought. The mind is everything. What we think is what we are and what we become. The whole world is the projection of our thoughts"

Our belief system is as mysterious as it is complex. We talk about and express ourselves through a set of beliefs which have been ingrained in us since birth and live by many beliefs, some of which are part of our subconscious. problems. If you believe you will lose your faculties as you age, you bring about early aging on yourself.

My bet would be that almost every community and the group of irrational elements in their belief systems. (If this is anything irrational another question)

Examples that come to mind, let's see if I can solve almost read each answer.

Software executives who seem to think that the methods of waterfall development can produce sometimes important innovations.

Voters who believe that their individual votes made a difference in the presidential election

Parents who believe their child is unique and special

Investors, they say, the calendar can market or exceeded the average performance through daily transactions

Several wise prophets and successful people affirm to the fact "Whether you believe you can, or instead you think you can't, either way, you are absolutely right." The Universe says and

In the American folklore there is a small but meaningful story among the Mahicans' native American tribe:

A grandfather and his grandson are sitting by a campfire on a cool, silent night, wrapped in warm clothing and gazing into the leaping flames. High on rocky ledges, a wildcat wail menacingly and loudly and another wildcat responds from a distance. Minutes later, the old man pauses between puffs on his pipe and says:

Grandson, here are two wildcats inside everyone. One is good, and the other is bad.

? Who are they, Grand dad? asks the interested, curious boy.

? They are fighting each other, says the old, wise man.

The boy considers this, then asks, why are they good and bad??

The good one is your love, your peace and your truth. The bad one is your fear, your anger and your bad habits

The fire crackles and sparks flare all around. The wildcat on the ridge wails again and the grandpa puffs happily on his pipe.

Finally, the boy asks: who will win, grandfather?

Well, says the old man, removing the pipe once more. The one that wins is the one you attend to.

Attend to the good in you. Connect to the source and you will be provided for.

You become what you think of most. What you feel follows you, what you believe builds around you.

If perhaps you are wondering: if we get what we focus on, why do we get so much of what we don't want? This is because we often focus most passionately on what we don't want, and our personal universe always grants our greatest passions. Be very precise and specific about what you want and do not put thought on what you don't want. Double negatives don't work. So, skip the "I don't want to be sick any more", largely because the word sick sticks out, so the ideal statement or thought would be " I am radiantly healthy right here and now and for always and can help others because I have perfect health and strength. If you are unhappy with your current job or the profession itself that you are in, steer clear from the thoughts of how you can get away from your horrible workplace. Instead visualize a happy workplace, a productive job which gives you satisfaction and gets you rewards of remuneration and recognition. you Here is the most strongly negative level of manifestation-thought process. Thinking you're not the creator of your life, but a victim of circumstances Blaming your condition on everything other than yourself, maybe the Heavens even your ancestry family, fate birth, parents, country, recession, accidents, sickness or the leaders. It's been always difficult. You are inherently incapable. You are a victim and life are a torment.... Are you this person?

Maybe better and positive at the next level, more evolved: you are sometimes the maker of your own life. You can influence some events, but mostly, external forces are too strong to fight off. You blame most of your condition on something other than yourself. You take some responsibility for what happens to you. You have some value some potential. Life is a struggle with a few highlights.... Are you like this?

Otherwise, let's take it higher: you are largely the maker of your life. You can influence most events, though sometimes external forces are too great. You take responsibility for most of your actions. You spend little time blaming others for painful events. You are a valuable person with faults. You have a lot of potential. Life is an interesting and often enjoyable challenge. Are you closer to this?

Now the highest: at the high standard of evolved level where the belief is that you are entirely the maker of your life. You are part of the great field of consciousness that has many adventures and many realities, including yours. You do not see your earth character as you, but as a spiritual being leading in an evolved human form. Your every thought, attitude and action are you're doing You are fully responsible, not only for your creations but for your response to your creations. You never blame or judge others for your experiences. Your inherent worth and value are increasing every day. Your life is a wonderful, joyful adventure on a smooth pathway, with a few downs but mostly ups all along.

Are you at this stage? These are standards of belief Whatever standard of manifestation-belief you own you will create the conditions that will prove you right. What you believe will keep happening for you and around you.

Mind manifests miracles the proven universal truth. Believe and accept optimism, happiness, health, love, peace, harmony, joy, fulfillment, self-love and self-worth and experience these in abundance once you decide to so empower your life. Growing up, I was admonished by my parents, which many children get to hear:" do not behave as if the whole world revolves around you". In fact, it does. Or rather, my world does. And so, does yours. Literally. As quantum physics is beginning to discover, there are an infinite number of energy worlds. Your consciousness experiences revolve around you, creating all that you know and experience and the trillion plus cells in your body and mind. You are the etheric body in an energy bubble of your making. Such energy field interacts with energy fields of others. Every direction you head in with your body, mind and aura, you create events and details of your experiences.

Chapter One

For over several decades now, many spiritual Masters, life coaches and certified practitioners have realized the power of spoken positive affirmations for nourishing and rejuvenating our mind, body and spirit. In the simplest terms, it is the practice of continually ingraining through thinking and of speaking positive intentions and affirmations of wellness, happiness, self-esteem and abundance in very specific terms of experiencing them right here in now and being grateful for all such goodness.

Keep repeating quietly in your mind the following as you go through your day:" Health, wealth, happiness. success flows through me right now and at all times". Repeat this as often as you can during the day and just before going to sleep and upon waking up. Soon you will begin experiencing better mood, start having a positive attitude towards people and things in life and overall find good things happening all the time.

Some of the best things in the world cannot be seen or touched, as none of them are outside objects. We were born with them and they exist within us. Enjoy them through your inner senses and with your hearts. The best and most exquisite are: optimism, happiness, hope, faith, peace, gratitude, love, joy, compassion and harmony. Reach within, tap into these vast resources and start living a better life.

The saying "We become how and what we think about ourselves" not only embraces our practical experiences, but is so all inclusive as to reach out to all conditions and circumstances of our lives We literally are what we think, and our characters and life patterns amount to the complete sum of all our thoughts. Our thoughts become our words over time, our words become feelings and slowly but surely our feelings manifest along positive or negative behavior patterns.

Just as plants grow from seeds, so do all our actions bloom from the in-ground seeds of thought, and could not have appeared without them. This applies equally to those acts called "spontaneous" and "unplanned " as well to those which are deliberately executed.

Actions are the blossom of thought, and happiness and unhappiness are their fruits

We receive sweet or bitter fruits based on the type of seeds we plant.

"Thoughts in your minds have made you as you are in body, mind and spirit. All what we are now started with our thoughts and finished up with their manifestations Whenever a person's mind carries evil thoughts, pain follows soon as a direct outcome

. Whenever we accept purity of thought, joy follows as surely as any law of nature We all grow through our thought process and create our own circumstances. Cause and effect is as absolute and undeviating in the hidden areas of thought as in the world of visible and material things. The human body consists of a combination of many biological systems made up with nearly 100 trillion cells. All humans are unique to the extent that there never was anybody exactly same nor will ever be the same as each of us and the combination of products, some good, some medium and some bad. They also manufacture the tools with which they build for themselves heavenly palaces of joy and strength and grace. By the right choice and true application of thought, people ascends to divine perfection; by the abuse and wrong application of thought, they descend below the level of beasts. Between these two extremes are all the grades of character, since people are their makers and masters. This may come as a profound revelation to some that we all have within ourselves the raw materials and tools to reshape ourselves in flesh and blood as the person we want to be and have within ourselves the mechanisms to live the lives of our dreams.

It is spiritually uplifting to realize our divine powers and prowess, of our oneness with the Universe with the fact that humans are masters of their destinies, that we mold our characters, and we make and shape their conditions, environment, and lives.

. through the laws of thought; Such discoveries are totally a matter of application, self-analysis, and experience.

Just as by much searching and mining, gold and diamonds are found, we all can find every truth connected with our being when we dig deep into the mine of our souls and find that we make our characters and create our lives and thus build our destinies. We will improve by watching, controlling, and altering our thoughts, tracing their effects upon ourselves, those around us and upon our life and circumstances, linking cause and effect by patient practice and investigation, and utilizing nature's every experience, even to the most trivial, everyday occurrence as a means of obtaining that knowledge of himself which is understanding, wisdom power. In this direction, as in no other, is the law is absolute.

People who seek, always find and those who try hard succeeding; sincere efforts are rewarded because with focus, dedication and consistent deeds dreams and desires are manifested.

Chapter Two

For centuries engineers and scientists have focused only on finding out what can be observed and calculated. The idea that thoughts have power was not scientifically acceptable. However, the facts are that thoughts do move sub-atomic particles around in our brains and our nervous systems. So, even though each neuron in the brain till now, cannot be seen and followed, the flow of neurons is tracked on MRI (magnetic resonance imaging) equipment. Such a measurable flow of neurons has a well-defined and predictable pattern of activity and they light up or "fire-up" in response to internal bodily functions or external stimuli which in turn effects precisely measurable blood flow and blood oxygen levels. The sophistication in scientific neurological measurements keeps evolving and improving, studies now   reveal changes in the behavior of the chemicals that bind neurons.

There is a basis for stating that neurotransmitter cells in your brain are listening to your thoughts and picking up on the feelings within you which your thoughts produce, which leads to the conclusion that thoughts do change your body functions and life outcomes. Come to think of the grandiose centuries' old wisdom of Archimedes, who said" Give me a long and strong lever, a fulcrum and a place to stand and I will move the earth". That was not only the law of physics but also the law of positive thinking. His talking about moving the earth at that time? How much more can your brain with scientific advancements imagine at present? Re-arranging distant galaxies?

Have you ever wondered why we feel defenseless at times when we read or listen to news about some dictators dominating their citizens? However there exists an easily accessible defense that goes beyond government weaponry and requires only effort to use. Within us is the power of our human mind. A recent research study focuses on the power of attraction to create wealth. Contrary to what many think, wealth accumulation isn't our most important goal. Using monetary and other resources for peace, improving the standard of living across borders and controlling global warming are more important issues when the entire world's future is at stake.

The human mind is like a garden, which may be thoughtfully cultivated or allowed to run wild; but whether cultivated or neglected, it will grow and take shape If no useful seeds are put into it, then an abundance of useless weed-seeds will spread within and will continue to produce many weeds. However quality seeds will result in beautiful flowers and harvests.

Just as gardeners cultivate their gardens, keeping them free from weeds, and growing flowers and fruits which they plan for, so may you tend the garden of your mind, weeding out all the wrong, useless, and impure thoughts and cultivating selectively flowers and fruits of correct useful, and pure thoughts. By pursuing this process, you will sooner or later discover that you are the master-gardener of your soul, the controller of your life. Within yourself you will realize the laws of thought and accurately understand, how the thought-forces and mind patterns flow through in the shaping of your character, destiny and circumstances, character Thought and character are aligned, and sincere character can only manifest itself through environment and circumstance, the outer conditions of a person's life will always be found to be coordinated with his/her inner state. This does not mean that a person's circumstances at any given time are a sign of his entire character, but that those circumstances are so intimately connected with some vital thought-elements within himself that, for the time being, they are indispensable to his development. By the law of our being, we are where and how we are living= built into our characters, thoughts have brought us there, and in the arrangement of our lives there are no elements of chance, but everything is the result of a law which is precise and all-pervasive. This is equally true of those who feel "out of harmony" with their surroundings as are those who are satisfied with themselves.

As progressive and evolving beings, we are placed where we are so that we may learn that we can grow; and as we learn the spiritual lessons that apply to our circumstance has for us, experiences evolve giving way to newer experiences.

At any time, if you feel buffeted by circumstances it will be long as you believe yourself to be creatures of outside conditions, shake yourself up to realize that you are your creative powers, and that you can command the hidden soil and seeds of your being out of which circumstances grow, you then become their rightful masters.

Since circumstances grow out of thought every man knows who has for any length of time practiced self-control and self-purification, for he will have noticed that the alteration in his circumstances has been in exact ratio with his altered mental condition. So true is this that when a man earnestly applies himself to remedy the defects in his character, and makes swift and marked progress, he passes rapidly through a succession of marked life changes.

The soul attracts that which it secretly harbors; that which it loves, and that which it fears; it reaches the height of its cherished aspirations; it falls to the level of its chastened desires, --and circumstances are how the soul receives its own.

Every thought-seed sown or allowed to fall into the mind, and to take root there, produces its own, blossoming sooner or later into act, and bearing its own harvest of opportunity and circumstance. Good thoughts bear good fruit, bad thoughts bad fruit.

The outer world of circumstance shapes itself to the inner world of thought, and both pleasant and unpleasant external conditions are factors, which make for the ultimate good of the individual. As the reaper of his own harvest, man learns both by suffering and bliss.

Following the inmost desires, aspirations, thoughts, by which he allows himself to be dominated, (pursuing threads of impure imagination or steadfastly walking the highway of strong and high endeavor), a man at last arrives at their fulfillment in the outer conditions of his life. The laws of growth and adjustment everywhere obtains.

A man does not come to the court or the jail by the tyranny of fate or circumstance, but by the pathway of groveling thoughts and base desires. Nor does a pure-minded man fall suddenly into crime by stress of any mere external force; the criminal thought had long been secretly fostered in the heart, and the hour of opportunity revealed its gathered power. Circumstances do not make the man; they reveal him to himself No such conditions can exist as descending into vice and its attendant sufferings apart from vicious inclinations, or ascending into virtue and its pure happiness without the continued cultivation of virtuous aspirations; and man, therefore, as the lord and master of thought, is the maker of himself and author of environment. Even at birth the soul comes to its own and through every step of its earthly pilgrimage it attracts those combinations of conditions which reveal itself, which are the reflections of its own purity and, impurity, its strength and weakness.

A. Trust the Universe: You are part of Divine creation and a magnificent expression of life. Embrace and accept your oneness with Divinity and repeat this in your thoughts and in words upon awakening, during the day and just before going to sleep:" I am one with Divinity and a magnificent expression of divine life. I am meant to be safe, secure and well in all possible ways at all times."

B. Keep focused on the positive, because whatever you focus on expands So expand on the positives of who you are and all that you have. Give thanks and be grateful for the fact that you are alive, be thankful that you have enough air to breathe and since you can breathe, you can smell the freshness of nature and the roses. Be thankful for the fact that the sun, air and water keep all humans, other live forms and vegetation alive. We all have so many things to be grateful about. the list would run into dozens or even hundreds and thousands. With a habit giving thanks and being grateful, you are increasing the flow of goodness that you receive. A very simple yet effective affirmation to repeat in your mind is: "I deserve the best, expect the best and receive the best right now and at all times". Say the above and believe that soul is all right and doing all right regardless of what is going on. Have ongoing faith in the Universe and you will be doing all right

There is so much abundance of what the Creator has granted you and the more you dwell on abundance and the goodness, the more you will receive." Conceive, believe and achieve" is not a mere slogan, it is the foundation for manifesting positive energy vibrations in the form of material things Divinity has shaped this law for all living beings from the dawn of creation forever.

Thought process is essential for creating our constantly evolving lives. Your thoughts completely give shape to our experiences and to material things in your lives.

Our lives are how we shape them with our thoughts. From the varied background of our thoughts and belief systems, we create everything in the way of who we are and all that we have. Sounds a bit fascinating and somewhat magical does [t it? But that's how it works; just by thinking of positive outcomes most of the times, we get them to manifest for us. It is logical that to direct our life outcomes, we must learn to control the nature of our recurring and dominant mental self-talk. Peaceful, harmonious, loving self-talk is achievable with a fair amount of focus and regular practice that we can continue to draw only positive events into our lives; all what we intend to have and experience for better living. The power of positive thinking can help you achieve everything, once you accept the truth that your thoughts create your reality. - right now, and into the future. In very practical ways and encouraging terms, we are entirely the true creators of our own world, every time and under all circumstances We ourselves shape our lives with our thoughts, words, beliefs and feelings. At first glance this logic may perhaps seem false, irrelevant or baseless because some can instantly point to events that were seemingly beyond your control: your birth circumstances, some illnesses, some accidents, your enemies, and that storm or hurricane that killed so many. Because no one says to themselves: it's okay that I sometimes get harmed, mugged or cheated."

So, let's get to the core of the universal truth with precision.: at mostly subconscious levels—starting long before birth and then with cumulative beliefs that were once subconscious¬ —you created them all: every event, detail and therefore all happenings in your lives.

Before birth we have chosen the pathways; during life we choose the lanes. One perfectly functional, healthy body, millions of arteries

To sum up, your mental patterns are truly your fixed life: genetics, ancestry, continent skin form, body shape and so like on as well as some predefined milestones like specific family members, a serious setback, a windfall inheritance or newly found fortunes. You then choose your arterial pathways every second of your waking lives—with your thinking. Simply put, your thoughts accumulate and become potent beliefs, the strongest ones operating at subconscious levels and affecting your next sequence in life choices. Little wonder that when something unpleasant happens, we think that we got a bad deal.

Let us recognize that we are an integral part of the great Universal magnificence. Ware expressions of the highest consciousness and we forget our greatness many times mainly that our dreams and desires can become reality with our thought power being attuned to Divinity. The earlier we realize this truth and take conscious control of our thoughts the earlier we declare our freedom and begin living fulfilled lives

Respond to the call to action, move away from mere existence towards joyous living.

Start believing that everyone is part of Divinity and truly magnificent., You are one with the ultimate source-the Super consciousness". These are proven values in spirituality for over 3,000 years and will continue remain valid to uplift humanity.

The truth above compliments the laws of contemporary science and metaphysics. Modern scientists, researching about the fundamental building blocks of the universe are discovering other laws. Here's one: both the presence and the behavior of subatomic particles depend on what is going on in the mind of the scientist".

"This may sound a bit fictional make believe but is really scientifically true and has been replicated many times. The implications are stunning. As one expert science researcher put it, "Physicists these days are uncovering untapped frontiers."

Conventional science assumes that consciousness arises from physical objects. Metaphysics states that the reverse is true too, something which Asian Hindu Masters have known for 3,000 years. No wonder that Buddha (the enlightened) put it this way: "All that we are is the result of what we have thought. The mind is everything. What we think is what we are and what we become. The whole world is the projection of our thoughts"

Our belief system is as mysterious as it is complex. We talk about and express ourselves through a set of beliefs which have been ingrained in us since birth and live by many beliefs, some of which are part of our subconscious. problems. If you believe you will lose your faculties as you age, you bring about early aging on yourself.

My bet would be that almost every community and the group of irrational elements in their belief systems. (If this is anything irrational another question)

Examples that come to mind, let's see if I can solve almost read each answer.

Software executives who seem to think that the methods of waterfall development can produce sometimes important innovations.

Voters who believe that their individual votes made a difference in the presidential election

Parents who believe their child is unique and special

Investors, they say, the calendar can market or exceeded the average performance through daily transactions

Several wise prophets and successful people affirm to the fact "Whether you believe you can, or instead you think you can't, either way, you are absolutely right." The Universe says and

In the American folklore there is a small but meaningful story among the Mahicans' native American tribe:

A grandfather and his grandson are sitting by a campfire on a cool, silent night, wrapped in warm clothing and gazing into the leaping flames. High on rocky ledges, a wildcat wail menacingly and loudly and another wildcat responds from a distance. Minutes later, the old man pauses between puffs on his pipe and says:

Grandson, here are two wildcats inside everyone. One is good, and the other is bad.

? Who are they, Grand dad? asks the interested, curious boy.

? They are fighting each other, says the old, wise man.

The boy considers this, then asks, why are they good and bad??

The good one is your love, your peace and your truth. The bad one is your fear, your anger and your bad habits

The fire crackles and sparks flare all around. The wildcat on the ridge wails again and the grandpa puffs happily on his pipe.

Finally, the boy asks: who will win, grandfather?

Well, says the old man, removing the pipe once more. The one that wins is the one you attend to.

Attend to the good in you. Connect to the source and you will be provided for.

You become what you think of most. What you feel follows you, what you believe builds around you.

If perhaps you are wondering: if we get what we focus on, why do we get so much of what we don't want? This is because we often focus most passionately on what we don't want, and our personal universe always grants our greatest passions. Be very precise and specific about what you want and do not put thought on what you don't want. Double negatives don't work. So, skip the "I don't want to be sick any more", largely because the word sick sticks out, so the ideal statement or thought would be " I am radiantly healthy right here and now and for always and can help others because I have perfect health and strength. If you are unhappy with your current job or the profession itself that you are in, steer clear from the thoughts of how you can get away from your horrible workplace. Instead visualize a happy workplace, a productive job which gives you satisfaction and gets you rewards of remuneration and recognition. you Here is the most strongly negative level of manifestation-thought process. Thinking you're not the creator of your life, but a victim of circumstances Blaming your condition on everything other than yourself, maybe the Heavens even your ancestry family, fate birth, parents, country, recession, accidents, sickness or the leaders. It's been always difficult. You are inherently incapable. You are a victim and life are a torment...... Are you this person?

Maybe better and positive at the next level, more evolved: you are sometimes the maker of your own life. You can influence some events, but mostly, external forces are too strong to fight off. You blame most of your condition on something other than yourself. You take some responsibility for what happens to you. You have some value some potential. Life is a struggle with a few highlights.... Are you like this?

Otherwise, let's take it higher: you are largely the maker of your life. You can influence most events, though sometimes external forces are too great. You take responsibility for most of your actions. You spend little time blaming others for painful events. You are a valuable person with faults. You have a lot of potential. Life is an interesting and often enjoyable challenge. Are you closer to this?

Now the highest: at the high standard of evolved level where the belief is that you are entirely the maker of your life. You are part of the great field of consciousness that has many adventures and many realities, including yours. You do not see your earth character as you, but as a spiritual being leading in an evolved human form. Your every thought, attitude and action are you're doing You are fully responsible, not only for your creations but for your response to your creations. You never blame or judge others for your experiences. Your inherent worth and value are increasing every day. Your life is a wonderful, joyful adventure on a smooth pathway, with a few downs but mostly ups all along.

Are you at this stage? These are standards of belief Whatever standard of manifestation-belief you own you will create the conditions that will prove you right. What you believe will keep happening for you and around you.

Mind manifests miracles the proven universal truth. Believe and accept optimism, happiness, health, love, peace, harmony, joy, fulfillment, self-love and self-worth and experience these in abundance once you decide to so empower your life. Growing up, I was corrected by my parents, which many children get to hear:" do not behave as if the whole world revolves around you". In fact, it does. Or rather, my world does. And so, does yours. Literally. As quantum physics is beginning to discover, there are an infinite number of energy worlds and our consciousness experiences revolve around you, creating all that you know and experience and the trillion plus cells in your body and mind. You are the etheric body in an energy bubble of your making. Such energy field interacts with energy fields of others. Every direction you head in with your body, mind and aura, you create events and details of your experiences.

Chapter One

For over several decades now, many spiritual Masters, life coaches and certified practitioners have realized the power of spoken positive affirmations for nourishing and rejuvenating our mind, body and spirit. In the simplest terms, it is the practice of continually ingraining through thinking and of speaking positive intentions and affirmations of wellness, happiness, self-esteem and abundance in very specific terms of experiencing them right here in now and being grateful for all such goodness.

Keep repeating quietly in your mind the following as you go through your day:" Health, wealth, happiness. success flows through me right now and at all times". Repeat this as often as you can during the day and just before going to sleep and upon waking up. Soon you will begin experiencing better mood, start having a positive attitude towards people and things in life and overall find good things happening all the time.

Some of the best things in the world cannot be seen or touched, as none of them are outside objects. We were born with them and they exist within us. Enjoy them through your inner senses and with your hearts. The best and most exquisite are: optimism, happiness, hope, faith, peace, gratitude, love, joy, compassion and harmony. Reach within, tap into these vast resources and start living a better life.

The saying "We become how and what we think about ourselves" not only embraces our practical experiences, but is so all inclusive as to reach out to all conditions and circumstances of our lives We literally are what we think, and our characters and life patterns amount to the complete sum of all our thoughts. Our thoughts become our words over time, our words become feelings and slowly but surely our feelings manifest along positive or negative behavior patterns.

Just as plants grow from seeds, so do all our actions bloom from the in-ground seeds of thought, and could not have appeared without them. This applies equally to those acts called "spontaneous" and "unplanned " as well to those which are deliberately executed.

Actions are the blossom of thought, and happiness and unhappiness are their fruits

We receive sweet or bitter fruits based on the type of seeds we plant.

"Thoughts in your minds have made you as you are in body, mind and spirit. All what we are now started with our thoughts and finished up with their manifestations Whenever a person's mind carries evil thoughts, pain follows soon as a direct outcome

. Whenever we accept purity of thought, joy follows as surely as any law of nature We all grow through our thought process and create our own circumstances. Cause and effect is as absolute and undeviating in the hidden areas of thought as in the world of visible and material things. The human body consists of a combination of many biological systems made up with nearly 100 trillion cells. All humans are unique to the extent that there never was anybody exactly same nor will ever be the same as each of us and the combination of products, some good, some medium and some bad. They also manufacture the tools with which they build for themselves heavenly palaces of joy and strength and grace. By the right choice and true application of thought, people ascends to divine perfection; by the abuse and wrong application of thought, they descend below the level of beasts. Between these two extremes are all the grades of character, since people are their makers and masters. This may come as a profound revelation to some that we all have within ourselves the raw materials and tools to reshape ourselves in flesh and blood as the person we want to be and have within ourselves the mechanisms to live the lives of our dreams.

It is spiritually uplifting to realize our divine powers and prowess, of our oneness with the Universe with the fact that humans are masters of their destinies, that we mold our characters, and we make and shape their conditions, environment, and lives.

. through the laws of thought; Such discoveries are totally a matter of application, self-analysis, and experience.

Just as by much searching and mining, gold and diamonds are found, we all can find every truth connected with our being when we dig deep into the mine of our souls and find that we make our characters and create our lives and thus build our destinies. We will improve by watching, controlling, and altering our thoughts, tracing their effects upon ourselves, those around us and upon our life and circumstances, linking cause and effect by patient practice and investigation, and utilizing nature's every experience, even to the most trivial, everyday occurrence as a means of obtaining that knowledge of himself which is understanding, wisdom power. In this direction, as in no other, is the law is absolute.

People who seek, always find and those who try hard succeeding; sincere efforts are rewarded because with focus, dedication and consistent deeds dreams and desires are manifested.

Chapter Two

For centuries engineers and scientists have focused only on finding out what can be observed and calculated. The idea that thoughts have power was not scientifically acceptable. However, the facts are that thoughts do move sub-atomic particles around in our brains and our nervous systems. So, even though each neuron in the brain till now, cannot be seen and followed, the flow of neurons is tracked on MRI (magnetic resonance imaging) equipment. Such a measurable flow of neurons has a well-defined and predictable pattern of activity and they light up or "fire-up" in response to internal bodily functions or external stimuli which in turn effects precisely measurable blood flow and blood oxygen levels. The sophistication in scientific neurological measurements keeps evolving and improving, studies now reveal changes in the behavior of the chemicals that bind neurons.

There is a basis for stating that neurotransmitter cells in your brain are listening to your thoughts and picking up on the feelings within you which your thoughts produce, which leads to the conclusion that thoughts do change your body functions and life outcomes. Come to think of the grandiose centuries' old wisdom of Archimedes, who said" Give me a long and strong lever, a fulcrum and a place to stand and I will move the earth". That was not only the law of physics but also the law of positive thinking. His talking about moving the earth at that time? How much more can your brain with scientific advancements imagine at present? Re-arranging distant galaxies?

Have you ever wondered why we feel defenseless at times when we read or listen to news about some dictators dominating their citizens? However there exists an easily accessible defense that goes beyond government weaponry and requires only effort to use. Within us is the power of our human mind. A recent research study focuses on the power of attraction to create wealth. Contrary to what many think, wealth accumulation isn't our most important goal. Using monetary and other resources for peace, improving the standard of living across borders and controlling global warming are more important issues when the entire world's future is at stake.

The human mind is like a garden, which may be thoughtfully cultivated or allowed to run wild; but whether cultivated or neglected, it will grow and take shape If no useful seeds are put into it, then an abundance of useless weed-seeds will spread within and will continue to produce many weeds. However quality seeds will result in beautiful flowers and harvests.

Just as gardeners cultivate their gardens, keeping them free from weeds, and growing flowers and fruits which they plan for, so may you tend the garden of your mind, weeding out all the wrong, useless, and impure thoughts and cultivating selectively flowers and fruits of correct useful, and pure thoughts. By pursuing this process, you will sooner or later discover that you are the master-gardener of your soul, the controller of your life. Within yourself you will realize the laws of thought and accurately understand, how the thought-forces and mind patterns flow through in the shaping of your character, destiny and circumstances, character Thought and character are aligned, and sincere character can only manifest itself through environment and circumstance, the outer conditions of a person's life will always be found to be coordinated with his/her inner state. This does not mean that a person's circumstances at any given time are a sign of his entire character, but that those circumstances are so intimately connected with some vital thought-elements within himself that, for the time being, they are indispensable to his development. By the law of our being, we are where and how we are living= built into our characters, thoughts have brought us there, and in the arrangement of our lives there are no elements of chance, but everything is the result of a law which is precise and all-pervasive. This is equally true of those who feel "out of harmony" with their surroundings as are those who are satisfied with themselves.

As progressive and evolving beings, we are placed where we are so that we may learn that we can grow; and as we learn the spiritual lessons that apply to our circumstance has for us, experiences evolve giving way to newer experiences.

At any time, if you feel buffeted by circumstances it will be long as you believe yourself to be creatures of outside conditions, shake yourself up to realize that you are your creative powers, and that you can command the hidden soil and seeds of your being out of which circumstances grow, you then become their rightful masters.

Since circumstances grow out of thought every man knows who has for any length of time practiced self-control and self-purification, for he will have noticed that the alteration in his circumstances has been in exact ratio with his altered mental condition. So true is this that when a man earnestly applies himself to remedy the defects in his character, and makes swift and marked progress, he passes rapidly through a succession of marked life changes.

The soul attracts that which it secretly harbors; that which it loves, and that which it fears; it reaches the height of its cherished aspirations; it falls to the level of its chastened desires, --and circumstances are how the soul receives its own.

Every thought-seed sown or allowed to fall into the mind, and to take root there, produces its own, blossoming sooner or later into act, and bearing its own harvest of opportunity and circumstance. Good thoughts bear good fruit, bad thoughts bad fruit.

The outer world of circumstance shapes itself to the inner world of thought, and both pleasant and unpleasant external conditions are factors, which make for the ultimate good of the individual. As the reaper of his own harvest, man learns both by suffering and bliss.

Following the inmost desires, aspirations, thoughts, by which he allows himself to be dominated, (pursuing threads of impure imagination or steadfastly walking the highway of strong and high endeavor), a man at last arrives at their fulfillment in the outer conditions of his life. The laws of growth and adjustment everywhere obtains.

We are shaped by our thoughts and over time, our thoughts attract people and things into our lives. The law of attraction has been known to mankind for centuries and philosophers, preachers and scholars have spoken and written about it extensively. Beyond a lifetime, the soul is reincarnated through future birth cycles is a theory held by several cultures in theworld.

Positive Thinking Mentor&Author Gautam Sharma (an intelligent, accomplished, capable, creative professional) has lived in Asia, Europe, Africa and now living in USA realizes and edifies positive thinking power of optimism and is sharing insights into human behavior and human potential through philosophical, psychological perspectives with the view of sharing mankind's centuries-old wisdom plus proven, research findings and to empower people worldwide. The author plans to utilize his strengths of professionalism, varied experience, creativity and communications' skills to publish the Empowerment Series on improvement, self-help topics. Thank you valued readers for your continuous support, contributions and your favorable feedback. Wishing everybody abundance of positive thinking and better living through the power of optimism. For all of us, may our self-confidence and self-esteem soar. Another book by the author:

Ohttps://www.amazon.com/POSITIVE-THINKING-OPTIMISM-Original-English-ebook/dp/B01HRY684S

CHAPTER FOUR

Ten practical ways to love, respect and honor yourself:

a. Be gentle and kind with yourself, accept yourself as you are and be your own biggest fan. These are the most important actions you can take for your health and happiness. Feel and fuel love for yourself everywhere always. Once you have built up a large reserve of self-love to become healthy, happy and fulfilled, you may start sharing and spreading love to your family, relatives, friends, communities close by or even far away. Regardless of your situation and circumstances, start to and practice truly loving and accepting everything about your body, mind and spirit. (literally affirming: I love and accept myself, right now and always) In your mind's eye, visualize your body, mind, spirit, being golden and glowing. Celebrate the fact that the Universe loves you- whoever and wherever you are, you are Divinity's exclusive creation. We all are special and precious since we all have something unique to offer, remind yourself that you are special, lucky and fortunate Fully embrace the essence of how important you are, identify with yourself fully. You will be amazed with the wellbeing, happiness and peace that loving yourself will bring to you. Continue to love yourself, love your life, love your world. Self-love is accepting and being true to oneself and it's being egoistic in any form self-love is keeping focused on improving your life first and realizing your true potential to begin with, you may choose to help others later. Trust and follow your intuition, instead of relying on somebody else's opinions. Research, analyze, collect feedbacks and take informed decisions yourself and if need be correct course, learn by trial and error and praise yourself for being independent and capable. Being kind to yourself, about your decision-making and being proud of your actions are cornerstones of secure self-love. trust your inner voice.

c Speak only good things about yourself. Most of us are not aware of how much we scold/minimize ourselves in thought or spoken word. In fact, very frequently many repeat degrading things like: should have done that, shouldn't have done that, not being good at something, some repeating dozens or even hundreds of things during the day "I should not have done this or that". This need correcting right now, so be gentle and kind to yourself as you continue to feel assured of your capacity and capabilities. and will be rewarded.

d. Speak only good things about others

Centuries old wisdom, in several cultures, postulates this axiom:" What others say about me is none of my business". Likewise, what you say about others defines nothing about them just everything about you. Criticizing and putting down other people/events sets up negative vibrations within us which affect our health negatively and creates unhappiness and dissatisfaction within yourself. It's best to learn to let go of rushing to judge and evaluate others. Others are entitled to their reasoning and actions and with their background, aptitude and knowledge are doing their best under the circumstances.

ebbed your best friend. Love your life, love your world.

How often do you encourage yourself to follow your dreams and dominate over your fears? How often do you act like your best friend? Let's love, respect and honor ourselves. We are so special and unique that there was noyon just like us till now and there will never be anyone exactly like us. make the most of it! Encourage and support yourself like best friend you can go.

f. Honor the divinity within yourself. Consider yourself beautiful, powerful and peaceful. Regardless of your perfections and imperfections, believe you are a miraculous presence of divinity on earth. With over 37 trillion cells within your body and mind functioning fulltime, you really are truly nature's special miracle The Universe created you to be perfect in every way and if you start believing this deep within, all cells will keep working in harmony for your happiness and success. make it perfect. in wonder and awe over how amazing you are? It is a miracle that you are even here, it is a miracle that you have a beautiful, functional body. Practice loving it. Where you see some imperfections, switch your thought to seeing an area that is a self-development opportunity and makes you a unique worked on instead see or an. Reach the point where you can look in the mirror at your body, no matter what state it is in and meaningfully say: "Wow I am glorious, glowing and awesome."

g. Remember to forgive yourself, forgive everybody for everything in all time and space and allow others to forgive you for everything. Repeat this every month. It is essential for each of us to be willing to forgive ourselves and others for everything in all spaces and times and allow all others to forgive us fevering as well in all spaces and times. By repeating this forgiveness process, repeated often, get released and free from negative patterns and start experiencing peace. everyone is just doing the best they can with the background, aptitude knowledge, in this way, periodically release and rid yourself of all negative patterns, cleanse yourself and stay in a state of peace.

h Reserve time for yourself alone. Take time out of your daily routine, even if it's just for a short spell, to do something just for yourself. Whether it's meditating, doing something creative or a short yoga session. Be in your own solitude in a relaxed state and you will experience alignment of your body, mind and soul-the perfect state for balance and harmony.

if. Be thankful and grateful to the Universe always. Make it a habit of being grateful and thankful for being alive, your body, your mind and spirit, your family and friends and all that sustains life form on earth and hundreds of things nature provides, which we may take for granted otherwise. Being grateful and thankful for all goodness brings more goodness in our lives.

CHAPTER FIVE

Nine practical ways to love, respect and honor the self:

a. Be kind to yourself, be your best friend. It's one of the most important actions you can take for happiness. It will help you spread love to your family, relatives, friends, close by or others even across the world only after you build enough love reserves within through loving yourself. Regardless of your situation and circumstances, start and practice truly loving everything about your body, mind and spirit. In your mind's eye, visualize your spirit, mind and body and mind to be golden and glowing. Celebrate the fact that the Universe loves you. We all are special, we all have something unique to offer, remind yourself that you are special, lucky and fortunate because you are loving, loved and lovable just because we were born, and we exist. Fully embrace the essence of how important you are, identify with yourself fully. You will be amazed with the wellbeing, happiness and peace that loving yourself will bring to you. Continue to love yourself, love your life, love your world. Self-love is accepting and being true to oneself and it's being egoistic in any form self-love is keeping focused on improving your life first and realizing your true potential to begin with, you may choose to help others later. Trust and follow your intuition, instead of relying on somebody else's opinions. Research, analyze, collect feedbacks and take informed decisions yourself and if need be correct course, learn by trial and error and praise yourself for being independent and capable. Being kind to yourself, about your decision-making and being proud of your actions are cornerstones of secure self-love.

trust your inner voice

c Speak only good things about yourself. We may not realize how much some of us degrade ourselves in thought or spoken word. In fact, very frequently some repeat belittling things like: should have done that, shouldn't have done that, not being good at something, some repeating dozens or even hundreds of things during the day "I should not have done this or that". This need correcting right now. Gently and be kind to yourself as you have been and will continue doing the best in your capacity. speak only good things about others. What you say about others says nothing about them and everything about you. Gossiping or making small talk about other people sends out bad vibes. It is also often an internal reflection of something deeper going on inside of you. It is never fair to judge others. This book gives10 practical ways to LOVE, RESPECT, HONOR YOURSELF and a PLAN TO BOOST SELF-CONFIDENCE & SELF-ESTEEM Do you sometimes wish what can make your life experiences mostly joyous and successful? Do you feel worthy and deserving enough to be a wonderful person having and enjoying a healthy and fulfilled lifestyle? How about boosting your self-worth and your true value to its optimal level? <bra><bra><bra><bra>Several types of people read this book: first those with healthy self-worth, others with low self-worth and the third kind are those with over inflated self-worth. Individuals with low and highly inflated self-worth are both narrow-minded; they are just different sides of the same bad coin Low self-worth often results in not bringing about what people want. On the other extreme, over inflated self-worth shows results faster and more easily but mostly with restrictions. The Author explains these facts clearly in the book. <bra><bra>Although interrelated, self-worth is not the same as self-esteem. Read about the differences and importantly how you can boost these in your life for health and happiness.

e) Be your best friend. Love your life, love your world. How often do you encourage yourself to follow your dreams and conquer your fears? How often do you act like your best friend? You only have this one life in this one body- make the most of it! Encourage and support yourself like a best friend and you will be surprised how far you can go.

f. Honor the divinity within yourself. Consider yourself beautiful, powerful and peaceful. Regardless of your perfections and imperfections, believe you are a miraculous presence of divination earth. With over 37 trillion cells in your body and mind functioning in unison, you really are nature's miracle. You are meant to be perfect in every way and if you start believing this, reality will truly make it prefetcher you ever wondered and got awed over how amazing you are? It is a miracle that you are even here, it is a miracle that you have a beautiful, functional body. Practice loving it. Where you see a flaw, switch perspectives and see the brighter side of your personality and the other side as an opportunity for improvement. Reach the point where you can look in the mirror at your body, no matter what state it is in and meaningfully say: "Wow I am wonderful as I am, I am awesome"

g. Begin to forgive yourself and others and be forgiven for everything. Itis essential for each of us to be willing to forgive ourselves and others for everything in all spaces and times and allow all others to forgive us fevering as well in all spaces and times. By repeating this forgiveness process, repeated often, get released and free from negative patterns and start experiencing peace. Forgive yourself and everybody else as everyone always does the best in whatever capacity and aptitude possible.

h Make time for yourself. Take time out of every day, even if it's just for a few minutes, to do something just for you. Whether it's meditating, doing something creative or taking a walk. Try to make this time 'alone' time so you can check in with yourself and tune into your own highest consciousness.

if Practice gratitude. Start by saying 'Thank You' to yourself for all your hard work, for your body, your life, your day and everything else in between. Learn how to be appreciative for what you have and give thanks for the life you have created so far. If you can't honor and respect what you have you close yourself off to receiving more. Once you can find the thanks in what you have, the doors of abundance will open wide to you.

1 Icing more. Once you can find the thanks in what you have, the doors of abundance will open wide to you.

pray for wellbeing, confidence, happiness and success. Through the power of prayer seek mental, physical, spiritual strength to remain in the state of grace.

CHAPTER FIVE

Plan of action for boosting self-confidence and self-esteem:

a). Become aware of your dominant thoughts with the purpose of guiding them towards positive thinking. Your dominant thoughts embed themselves in your subconscious to create your beliefs and habits which translate into your actions and in turn create your reality. Give your thoughts constant review seeking to stay happy and upbeat. Give yourself such appositive boost of positivity from time to time. Regardless of the present circumstances, replace negative thoughts gently, lovingly with uplifting, joyous, laughing, rejoicing thoughts-thoughts of love, peace, hope, compassion, winning, celebrating.

b). Write down, in order of importance, all your major strengths and your significant achievements till date. If you need prompting, ask a relative or a close friend to help with inputs for recalling traits and events and cover all the major plus points in this. Rewrite this list and read it to yourself every morning, because repeating these in thought and spoken word will make a deep imprint of your positive aspects on your subconscious c). Think positively about yourself. Remind yourself that, despite your problems, you are a special, worthy and valued person, and that you deserve to feel good and content about yourself. Remind yourself that the universe loves you and you love the universe and that you are beautiful and peaceful in body, mind and spirit just as you are. Your presence makes a valuable difference in the world just because you exist. Remove from your consciousness and permanently delete all negative thoughts about yourself such as 'I am an under achiever, 'I never do anything right', or 'Not many really like me. Instead keep repeating:" I am important, loving and loved, "I make a valuable difference in the world. Build yourself up and stay positively expanded. In metaphysical terms, you are much bigger than an average human, in fact a magnificent expression of divinity here on earth.

d) Choose to have nutritious foods part of a healthy, balanced diet. Slow down while eating as meal times are special, even if you are eating alone. Switch off the computer/laptop/television, feel good by setting the table and eat food slowly with relish and gratitude.

e). Make it a regular habit to get enough sleep (aim for 7/8 hours). Encourage thoughts of gratitude and thankfulness just before sleeping and right after waking up.

f) Clean and groom yourself regularly by taking showers, brushing your teeth and your hair, trimming your nails, keeping neat and clean, wear clean clothes and use deodorants and fragrances where appropriate.

Dressing up with cleanliness, finesse and finery makes you feel extra good about yourself. Within your wardrobe choice and budgets, put on nicest, cleanest, fashionable clothes-it all helps a lot in boosting your self-esteem.

g) Put on suitable clothes and shoes to exercise daily by walking every day, either outdoors or on a treadmill and work up a sweat with cardio -workouts several times a week, keeping within your doctors' advice.

h) Make it a habit of reducing your stress levels with simple practical methods. In their simplest form, teach yourself relaxation exercises, deep, outdoor breathing, any suitable form of meditation and practice all these as often as you can. You may find relaxation also with hobbies as tending to and watering your plants or playing with and grooming your pet or whatever hobby that makes you relaxed and peaceful.

if) Take out items that remind you of your achievements and happy, memorable times, of people special to you and display them where you and others can view them often.

j) Add on to your routine some more things that you enjoy. Find time to indulge in at least one or two pleasurable things every day.

k). Take up creative activities: any enjoyable form of music, dancing, art, literary pursuits will bring out hidden, normally unexpressed talents and help you communicate with your intrinsic goodness and communicate with others lovingly. Take part in local community groups, courses, programs accessible to you for such pastimes.

Find interest in your friends' and community activities to lend a hand and help others by using your talents, energy, enthusiasm. Make some time for these late evenings or on weekends, because taking interest in others and helping them out will bring a sense of satisfaction to them and to yourself. Also remember that what goes around, comes around: you will receive attention, gratitude and respect from others.

always be friendly, kind and gentle to yourself by appreciating yourself, being happy with all decisions that you have taken. In fact, yourself for taking the best decisions in the light of your aptitude, training and circumstances. Celebrate important achievements and milestones and be proud of your value and worth.

Keep company of people who are important in life and mean a lot for you. Also reach out to network to meet more likeminded people and expand your contacts and connections. Social media communities are a possible start to get introductions and accept more friends into your circle n). Stay away from negative people who draw you down and with whom you cannot build up healthy relationships. You have started focusing on family, friends and more likeminded people, so you can let go ties with people you are not comfortable with.

. Once you have focused on the stages above, by keeping an open mind (stage 4), you will start feeling valuable and worthy (stage 5) and the vibrations that your mental and emotional states create will move you to action towards what you desire and have visualized. (stage 6)

On a broader note, have you realized that he ten most prized things on earth cannot be seen or touched, as none of them are external things. We were born with them and they exist within us. You can feel them through your inner senses and with your hearts. The best and the most beautiful are optimism, happiness, hope, peace, faith, gratitude, love, kindness, peace and confidence. So, with concerted actions reach within, tap into your abundant resources and empower your lives.

. A saying in several languages" when the going gets tough, the tough get going" is so true in everyday context that many positive, optimistic people get their inspiration from it to just pick themselves up, dust themselves off and keep going in case of a stumble or a fall.

Normally people are open to self-improvement, but not willing to try out logical suggestions to bring about improved life experiences. Change is a law of nature and learning by trial and error is a practical methodology. the better; stuck in their Those who are open to putting in efforts are normally rewarded by getting what they had wished for. Goals could vary from average standards of health, wealth and happiness to the highest and loftiest

Self-esteem relates to our principles and our ideals

Ideals are deeply held beliefs that guide us towards what is

right as against what is wrong

There are a wide range of ideals and understandably belief systems are subjective, because all people measure life experiences with their own perspectives. Every person's point of view is unique and, as a result, there are differing ideals for each of us which guide us uniquely through life.

There are ideals that are positively benevolent, others mid-range and yet others even harmfully negative. There is love, compassion as against being mean or hateful. There is charity and there is robbery. There is happiness and grief. Others are support for family, community, work, tolerance, respect, and hundreds of other ideals.

We are guided and propelled by our ideals throughout our lives. up of our set our ideals. Our individual combination of ideals has restricted us or glorified us right from our formative years and we have modified and added others over time.

Ideals are important for all of us because they are the set of guidelines which shape our priorities and reactions and hence our character and uniqueness. We must align our words and actions to our ideals so that we feel content, confident and satisfied.

They let us know what is important to us and help prioritize areas of action. ideals help you gain clarity and focus in your life. ideals help you make decisions—which leads us to principles.

Why are principles important too?

Correctly defined, principles are a firm adherence to a code of especially moral or artistic ideals.

To be a person of principles we must live up to the ideals we hold to be important. (Again, notice how subjective this all is—the ideals we hold to be important.)

With principles, it doesn't matter what your ideals are. It matters whether you live up to them.

Principles are connections between your ideals and your actions.

This is how ideals and principles are related to self -esteem

The world we live in takes for granted expect certain things from us, yet we are the ones who choose whether we personalize external social ideals and accept them as our own.

An extensive study conducted by a California University has shown that people have a range of ideal s and 60 percent are convinced that what's right for each person is the average norm for society regardless what others think even if others' views are totally divergent. "this supplements age old wisdom of "Let all be guided by a correct set of ideals, based on how society and community groups have evolved in different parts of the world."" There is no single right or wrong set of ideals but many different sets just as there are many paths to human growth, development and enlightenment".

Each of us has many ideals. Not all our ideals are as important to us at the same time. Over the years we change, our priorities in life changes and accordingly our ideals change- some get dropped and others get added to our own top ten ideals' list.

The more important our ideals, the more they will affect our self-esteem.

Let's analyze at how some ideals conflict with each other. Family value or family ideal being a common priority with many clashes with work values or ideals of excelling at the workplace. Through focusing on work a bit extra draws us away from family ideal, hence conflicting and upsetting a happy state of mind.

The more our work ideals are accomplished, the more principles we have with reference to that ideal. On the other hand, I am not living my family value with as much principles as I would like to. When there's such a conflict between the two it amounts to a loss of principles.

That depletion of principles is the cause of lowered self-esteem.

Check to see if you have low self-esteem, that shows you need to go back to your ideals and rearrange your life to get back to living with principles based on what matters to you.

The good news is that low self-esteem can be corrected. For the family and work ideals example above, you can balance with a 50-50 or a 60-40 percent involvement, spending equal amount of time between both and achieve satisfaction in both areas- a sensitive balancing act but it keeps you happy and successful.

Principles are built from successive smaller but consistent actions. Little changes can amount to big changes. Small advances, a little bit Avery time, will make big diffcrences

For a paradigm shift to super self-confidence and self-esteem, start believing that you have dormant powers to bring about miracles, that you are worthy, valid and valuable. Since you exist Believe that you are born to be a confident, accomplished person for doing good for the world and for humanity at large. I invite you to repeat to yourself several times these sentences with me

I.   you   are   worthy   and   valuable

2.You will enjoy good things and get through everything else.

3.   You   are   beautiful,   loving   and   loved

4. You can find peace, happiness and contentment

5. You have the power and the will to persist and carry on.

Your core entity of existence makes you a worthwhile, important and valued regardless of factors such as looks, brains, status and wealth   are secondary and peripheral Start believing that you are valid, valued and valuable There has never been nor will ever be any person exactly like   you, You are unique and special. Repeat this in your own mind several times every day: I have everything that I need, I am complete in every way always, I am becoming more and more aware of my own worth and value I easily handle situations of all kinds as and when they arise, my self-confidence increases every day and I am super self-confident and have very high self-esteem. Research has proven over years that for respecting and honoring the self the following factors are important:

A. Accept yourself in totality- all parts, the good, the bad, the indifferent, your triumphs, your failures- everything.

Bastron belief in the self: This trait is associated with both a diverse thought process, i.e. creativity as well as brainstorming, and the related idea that humans are complete within themselves. Being confident is all about knowing that humans have powerful resources within themselves, in metaphysical terminology" We are complete in every way" and "We have everything we need within ourselves"/

How can self-confidence be increased? Techniques which may help increase divergent thinking are brainstorming, maintaining a lifestyle journal, free writing and mind hierarchical analysis. These laceratingly worth exploring and these have worked in numerous instances where pursued them with persistence and faith in their efficacy.

Diligence: People who are diligent can be depended upon for efficiency and integrity since they have a strong sense of purpose and duty towards getting work at hand completed.

One way to increase diligence is to get people to integrate within cohesive relationships like marriage or close families or work teams or even community groups. Extensive studies in several countries over two decades have shown that as people strengthen their family, work group or social commitments, they become, over time, more diligent, purposeful and focused on achieving the higher good for all concerned.

3. Evaluating oneself: this covers traits like mental, emotional balance and situational self-control. The goal is to keep boosting balance and self-control which in turn boosts self-esteem.

There are ways to enhance this. Increased power of control can be achieved with the use of psychotherapy. The psychotherapy option is backed by the principle that our mindset on life is largely related to the way we perceive what happens to us and others – the basis of experiences. Changing our outlook about experiences changes way we judge ourselves.

The above points have been valid for decades in most societies over decades and wherever they don't apply in totality is because social standards have been radically unusual.

Positivity along the following lines is ideal for self-improvement and can help you boost confidence.

1. Enhanced self-assuredness: basically, means confidence in the self and one's ability to achieve defined goals.

Keep your good experiences and achievements close to your heart and in your mind. Let your negative experiences and failures drift away and disappear into nothingness. Make it a habit of enhancing joyfulness and deleting uneasiness until it becomes second nature for you.

Make it a daily mantra that you are absorbing more and more self-confidence for ongoing happiness and success.

1. Write down in clear terms what you plan to do and have committed to achieve. Set down clear goals and a short plan of action.

2. Announce to other people that you will complete all tasks you have committed to within the pre-set time frame

3. React to critical feedback with a peaceful response. For all negativity coming to you, evaluate an objective and balanced response and resolution and act with self-confidence. Having realized above that you have all powers needed within yourself, you can retain

Expanding your skill set will help build confidence because it goes right to the source of being more capable, worthy and valuable. Earlier you may have felt inadequate at work and uncertain because you couldn't complete work with insufficient training, did not have the proper work skills for efficient `   performance. However, with do it yourself online courses, work seminars and online support you can find yourself competent, complete and capable of meeting your work requirements deadlines. Some of these mentioned above these are constructive ways of improving your work efficiency and improving your self-confidence and self-esteem.

6. Increase your knowledge

Another avenue for building confidence by learning.

Love, respect and honor the self for relationships.

Healthy, secure relationships are a two way and a reciprocal recess. Each person first loves themselves and then the other person in equal measures and they together have a happy, meaningful, ongoing relationships

This book recommends that people focus on and understand their needs first and by doing so they remain in an attractive state and can attract vibrant, positive relationships into their lives. Until you love yourself, others cannot love you. Simply put 2 matched people start by loving themselves and then start loving the other, forming a strong bond. Let's address 3 main rules to follow: respect yourself, love yourself and take care of yourself. Let's address each of these in order. Positive actions understanding their own needs before they rely on others to make them happy. first so you can be in great shape to attract positive, vibrant people into your life and share great relationships. The good news is that there are many straightforward things you can do today to begin the process of respecting and loving yourself. The three main areas we'll look at are respect, loving ourselves and taking care of ourselves.

Different sets of psychologists and psychotherapists are divided over how individuals acquire their patterns of respecting, loving and honoring themselves but what is agreed upon is that we picked these up mostly from our parents and the events and circumstances during our formative years. Self-respect is how you would like to be treated. Ideally, we should define our own preferences and let others know through verbal or nonverbal communication, our main preferences on how we would like to be treated. We start off by treating others with empathy, understanding and politeness and then define how we, in turn, would like to be addressed, treated and communicated with. We do all this while creating conditions that will make both us and other people feel good about themselves and the

Where did you learn what respect means? It was likely from your family or social circles, but these aren't always reliable sources for productive behaviors. It seems everyone has a different definition of respect based on their own experience, which leaves everyone guessing and doing different things that may or may not lead to respectful relationships. Some people know how to ask for respect but don't know how to give it; others can't ask for it at all. The key point is for you to define respect in a way that works for you and that you can clearly communicate to others. For our purposes, a working definition of respect is creating the conditions that lead to both people feeling great about themselves and each other. People who are respectful allow other people to be themselves, encourage them to grow, celebrate their triumphs, soothe their disappointments, listening to them and support them unconditionally. Respect is reciprocal, functions as the basis of strong relationships and is practiced equally by all parties involved.

A productive starting point in the quest to find respect is figuring out what you want out of your relationships and how you would like to be treated. Develop a definition of respect that works for you and that you can clearly communicate to others. Think in terms of communicating who you are as a person and what is important to you. As you've probably noticed, people aren't mind readers - we must tell them what we want. It's best to assume that people will only treat us how we ask them to. You literally show people how to treat you through your actions. If you act like a doormat you will attract people who will treat you like one. If you are healthy and balanced, you will attract the same.

The second phase of self-care is learning how to love yourself. In general, people who love themselves are balanced, accepting, giving and possess self-knowledge. They seem comfortable in their own skin. A helpful tool you can use to figure out who you are is to honestly assess your situation and write it down. Make a list of the things in your life that make you feel wonderful and the ones that bring you down. Take some time to reflect on what you wrote down to help you begin examining who you are. Pick one item from the negative side that you want to work on and commit to doing something about it today. Congratulate yourself because you have now started the process of working on self-love.

As you've probably guessed, loving yourself is about self-reflection and doing things that lead to positive outcomes. If you have trouble reflecting on yourself, you may ask yourself some key questions to help you start the process. What is my passion in life? What are the things I do well? What are the areas I can improve? What do I want out of relationships? What is my part in creating great relationships? Self-love grows from understanding who we are and working through the things that block our ability to love ourselves. For example: if you have difficulty committing in a relationship it may stem from something inside you that blocks you from accepting or giving love. If you identify what is blocking you it suddenly gives you a lot of power to change what you are doing.

Treating yourself well is the final step we'll examine. Many of us have had our hearts broken by a significant other, a parent, a friend, a relative or a coworker. You get to choose whether you learn from these events or let them hold you back. It's normal to feel hurt but how you deal with pain will determine whether you take care of yourself or not. You can choose to stay stuck in pain and misery or elect to be kind to your heart. The next time you find yourself feeling pain inside ask yourself some questions that will help you take care of it. What is hurting me? What can I do to improve how I feel and take care of myself? What can I do to interrupt the pattern that keeps my heart hurting? When you discover where your pain comes you can soothe yourself rather than letting the hurt continue indefinitely.

You possess an amazing power to respect and love yourself, but it is a skill that requires practice and conscious thought. As with anything in life, you only become expert at something if you strive to master it. You will also experience great joy in your life and relationships as you discover what respect means to you, practice self-love and treat yourself with kindness.

Ten practical ways to love, respect and honor yourself:

a. Be kind to yourself, be your best friend

It's one of the most important actions you can take for happiness. It will help you spread love to your family, relatives, friends, close by or others even across the world only after you build enough love reserves within through loving yourself. Regardless of your situation and circumstances, start and practice truly loving everything about your body, mind and spirit. In your mind's eye, visualize your spirit, mind and body and mind to be golden and glowing. Celebrate the fact that the Universe loves you. We all are special, we all have something unique to offer, remind yourself that you are special, lucky and fortunate because you are loving, loved and lovable just because we were born, and we exist. Fully embrace the essence of how important you are, identify with yourself fully. You will be amazed with the wellbeing, happiness and peace that loving yourself will bring to you. Continue to love yourself, love your life, love your world.

Self-love is accepting and being true to oneself and it's being egoistic in any form. Self-love is keeping focused on improving your life first and realizing your true potential to begin with, you may choose to help others later. Trust and follow your intuition, instead of relying on somebody else's opinions. Research, analyze, collect feedbacks and take informed decisions yourself and if need be correct course, learn by trial and error and praise yourself for being independent and capable. Being kind to yourself, about your decision-making and being proud of your actions are cornerstones of secure self-love.

trust your inner voice

c Speak only good things about yourself

We may not realize how much some of us belittle ourselves in thought or spoken word. In fact, very frequently some repeat belittling things like: should have done that, shouldn't have done that, not being good at something, some repeating dozens or even hundreds of things during the day "I should not have done this or that". This need correcting right now. Gently and be kind to yourself as you have been and will continue doing the best in your capacity.

d. Speak only good things about others

What you say about others says nothing about them and everything about you. Gossiping or making small talk about other people sends out bad vibes. It is also often an internal reflection of something deeper going on inside of you. It is never fair to judge others.

ebbed your best friend. Love your life, love your world

How often do you encourage yourself to follow your dreams and conquer your fears? How often do you act like your best friend? You only have this one life in this one body- make the most of it! Encourage and support yourself like a best friend and you will be surprised how far you can go.

f. Honor the divinity within yourself

From time to time, it helps to pause, feel connected to the Universe and give your self-esteem a boost. Consider yourself beautiful, powerful and peaceful. Regardless of your perfections and imperfections, believe you are a miraculous presence of divinity on earth. Imagine and believe that with over 37 trillion cells in your body and mind functioning in harmony, you really are nature's miracle. You are meant to be perfect in every way and if you start believing this, the minor aches and pains should disappear to begin with and over time you will realize your consciousness opening to higher states of mind, body, spirit wellbeing. Ever realize how awesome you truly are? It is a miracle that you are here and alive in this time and space, it is a miracle that you have a functional body. Start practicing loving it. Where you see a blemish, switch the thought to see your uniqueness, a self-development opportunity personality or an opportunity. Try and get to the stage where you can look in the mirror at your body, no matter how your body is, at print, repeat to yourself: "Wow I am beautiful. "This fake it, till you make it mirrorwork exercise will bring out wonders in your life. Go ahead express your self-worth.

g. Begin to forgive yourself and others and be forgiven for everything

Itis essential or each of us to be willing to forgive ourselves and others for everything in all spaces and times and allow all others to forgive us fevering as well in all spaces and times. By repeating this forgiveness process, repeated often, get released and free from negative patterns and start experiencing peace. everyone is just doing the best they can with the knowledge they have.

h Make time for yourself

Take time out of every day, even if it's just for a few minutes, to do something just for you. Whether it's meditating, doing something creative or taking a bath. Try to make this time 'alone' time so you can check in with yourself and tune into the hum of your soul.

I. Be thankful and grateful always

Make it a habit of being grateful and thankful for being alive, your body, your mind and spirit, your family and friends and all that sustains life form on earth and hundreds of things nature provides, which we may take for granted otherwise. Being grateful and thankful for all goodness brings more goodness in our lives. Nine practical ways to love, respect and honor the self:

a. Be kind to yourself, love yourself and be your best admirer.

It's one of the most important actions you can take for happiness. It will help you spread love to your family, relatives, friends, close by or others even across the world only after you build enough love reserves within through loving yourself. Regardless of your situation and circumstances, start and practice truly loving everything about your body, mind and spirit. In your mind's eye, visualize your spirit, mind and body and mind to be golden and glowing. Celebrate the fact that the Universe loves you. We all are special, we all have something unique to offer, remind yourself that you are special, lucky and fortunate because you are loving, loved and lovable just because we were born, and we exist. Fully embrace the essence of how important you are, identify with yourself fully. You will be amazed with the wellbeing, happiness and peace that loving yourself will bring to you. Continue to love yourself, love your life, love your world. Self-love is accepting and being true to oneself and it's being egoistic in any form self-love is keeping focused on improving your life first and realizing your true potential to begin with, you may choose to help others later. Trust and follow your intuition, instead of relying on somebody else's opinions. Research, analyze, collect feedbacks and take informed decisions yourself and if need be correct course, learn by trial and error and praise yourself for being independent and capable. Being kind to yourself, about your decision-making and being proud of your actions are cornerstones of secure self-love.

trust your inner voice

c Speak only good things about yourself

We may not realize how much some of us belittle ourselves in thought or spoken word. In fact, very frequently some repeat belittling things like: should have done that, shouldn't have done that, not being good at something, some repeating dozens or even hundreds of things during the day "I should not have done this or that". This need correcting right now. Gently and be kind to yourself as you have been and will continue doing the best in your capacity.

d. Speak only good things about others

What you say about others says nothing about them and everything about you. Gossiping or making small talk about other people sends out bad vibes. It is also often an internal reflection of something deeper going on inside of you. It is never fair to judge others.

ebbed your best friend. Love your life, love your world

How often do you encourage yourself to follow your dreams and conquer your fears? How often do you act like your best friend? You only have this one life in this one body- make the most of it! Encourage and support yourself like a best friend and you will be surprised how far you can go.

f. Honor the divinity within yourself

Consider yourself beautiful, powerful and peaceful. Regardless of your perfections and imperfections, believe you are a miraculous presence of divinity on earth. With over 37 trillion cells in your body and mind functioning in unison, you are really nature's miracle. You are meant to be perfect in every way and if you start believing this, you will notice improvements within yourself. in wonder and awe over how amazing you are? It is a miracle that you are even here, it is a miracle that you have a beautiful, functional body. Be thankful and grateful for your body and mind and begin loving these as priceless possessions. If you notice any imperfections, embrace them as making you special and opportunities for improvement. It will take some practice but can look in the mirror at your body, no matter what state it is in and meaningfully say: "Wow I am beautiful and valuable"

g. Begin to forgive yourself and others and be forgiven for everything

Itis essential or each of us to be willing to forgive ourselves and others for everything in all spaces and times and allow all others to forgive us fevering as well in all spaces and times. By repeating this forgiveness process, repeated often, get released and free from negative patterns and start experiencing peace. everyone is just doing the best they can with the knowledge they have.

h Make time for yourself

Take time out of every day, even if it's just for a few minutes, to do something just for you. Whether it's meditating, doing something creative or taking a bath. Try to make this time 'alone' time so you can check in with yourself and tune into the hum of your soul.

I. Practice gratitude

Start by saying 'Thank You' to yourself for all your hard work, for your body, your life, your day and everything else in between. Learn how to be appreciative for what you have and give thanks for the life you have created so far. If you can't honor and respect what you have you close yourself off to receiving more. Once you can find the thanks in what you have, the doors of abundance will open wide to you.

1 Icing more. Once you can find the thanks in what you have, the doors of abundance will open wide to you.

Pray for wellbeing, confidence, happiness and success. Through the power of prayer seek mental, physical, spiritual strength to remain in the state of grace. Many people are looking only for big, awesome experiences to help others, but they tend to miss out on extending and sharing daily acts of empathy and helpfulness. Fortunately, however, they are so taken up with rendering what they call little services, that they have no time to worry because the big opportunities do not come their way. Love, help others, make a positive impact on others' lives in a small, medium or a big way, whichever you are capable of and have the time for.

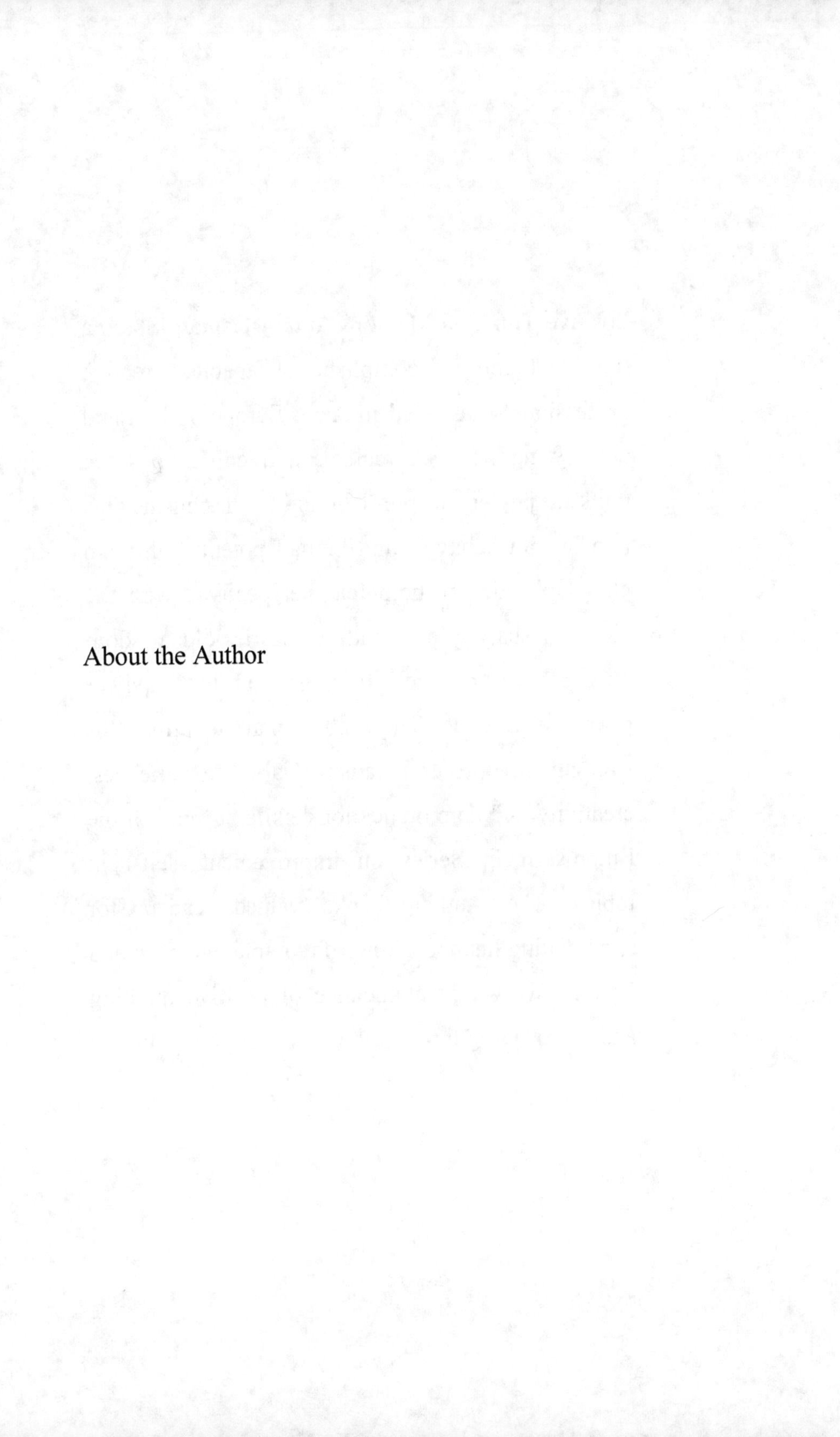

About the Author

Positive Thinking Mentor&Author Gautam Sharma (an intelligent, accomplished, capable, creative professional) has lived in Asia, Europe, Africa and now living in USA realizes and edifies positive thinking power of optimism and is sharing insights into human behavior and human potential through philosophical, psychological perspectives with the view of sharing mankind's centuries-old wisdom plus proven, research findings and to empower people worldwide. The author plans to utilize his strengths of professionalism, varied experiences, creativity and communications' skills to publish the Empowerment Series on improvement, self-help topics. The Author thanks valued readers for appreciating his books, their favorable feedback and Wishes everybody abundance of positive thinking and better living through the power of optimism.

Plan of action for boosting self-confidence and self-esteem:

a). Become aware of your dominant thoughts with the purpose of guiding them towards positive thinking. Your dominant thoughts embed themselves in your subconscious to create your beliefs and habits which translate into your actions and therefore create your reality. Give your thoughts constant reviews to stay happy and upbeat... Regardless of the present circumstances, replace negative thoughts gently, lovingly with uplifting, joyous, laughing, rejoicing thoughts- thoughts of love, peace, hope, compassion, winning, celebrating.

b). Write down, in order of importance, all your major strengths and your significant achievements till date. If you need prompting, ask a relative or a close friend to help with inputs for recalling traits and events and make this list complete with everything significant. Rewrite this list and read it to yourself every morning, because repeating these in thought and spoken word will make a deep imprint of your positive aspects on your subconscious c). Think positively about yourself. Remind yourself that, regardless of your failures, you are a special, worthy and valued person, and that you deserve to feel good and content about yourself. Remind yourself that the Universe loves you universe and that you are beautiful and peaceful in body, mind and spirit just as you are. Your presence makes a valuable difference in the world just because you exist. Remove by deleting from your consciousness all negative thoughts about yourself such as 'you are an under achiever, 'you never do anything right', or 'Not many people really like me. Instead keep repeating:" I am important, loving and loved, "I make a valuable difference in the world. Build yourself up and stay positively expanded. In metaphysical terms, you are much bigger than an average human being, in fact you are a magnificent expression of divinity

d) Choose to have fresh, nutritious food as part of a healthy, balanced diet. Slow down while eating as meal times are special, even if you are eating on your work desk or alone. Switch off the computer/laptop/television, feel good by clearing the table and eat food slowly with relish and gratitude.

e). Make it a regular habit to get enough sleep (aim for 7to8 hours). Instill joyous thoughts, thoughts of gratitude and thankfulness just before sleeping and right after waking up.

f) Clean and groom yourself regularly and well by taking showers, brushing your teeth and your hair, trimming your nails, keeping well-groomed and smelling fresh, wear clean clothes and use deodorants and fragrances as appropriate.

Dressing up with style, finesse and finery will make you feel extra good about yourself. Within your wardrobe choices and budgets, put on the nicest, cleanest, fashionable clothes- all this will boost your self-esteem right away.

g) At leisure time, put on suitable clothes and shoes to exercise daily by walking every day, either outdoors or on a treadmill and work up a sweat with cardio -workouts several times a week, keeping within your doctors' advice.

h) Make it a habit of reducing your stress levels with simple practical methods. In their simplest form, teach yourself relaxation exercises, deep, outdoor breathing, any suitable form of meditation and practice all these as often as you can. You may find relaxation also with hobbies as tending to and watering your plants or playing with and grooming your pets or whatever hobby that makes you relaxed and peaceful.

if). Bring out items that remind you of your achievements and your happiest, memorable times, o people special to you and display them where you and others can view them often-these are to focus on joyous memories and happy thoughts.

j). Add on to your routine some more things that you enjoy. Find time to indulge in at least one or two pleasurable things every day.

k). Take up creative activities: any enjoyable form of music, dancing, art, literary pursuits will bring out hidden, normally unexpressed talents and help you communicate with your intrinsic goodness and help communicate with others lovingly. Take part in your circle of friends, local community groups, courses, programs accessible to you for such or similar pastimes.

k. Take interest in your friends' and community activities to lend a hand and help others out by using your talents, energy, enthusiasm, your caring, sharing spirit. Make some time for these late evenings or on weekends, because taking interest in others and helping them out will bring a sense of satisfaction to them and to yourself. Also remember that what goes around, comes around. Giving and receiving is an ongoing circle of positive, beneficial energy- you will receive attention, gratitude and respect from others.

always be friendly, kind and gentle to yourself by appreciating yourself, being happy with all decisions that you have taken. In fact, yourself for taking the best decisions in the light of your aptitude, training and circumstances. Celebrate important achievements and milestones and be proud of your value and worth.

Keep company of people who are important in life and mean a lot for you. Also reach out to network to meet more likeminded people and expand your contacts and connections. Social media communities are a possible start to get introductions and accept more friends into your circle n). Stay away from negative people who draw you down and with whom you cannot build up healthy relationships. You have started focusing on family, friends and more likeminded people, so you can let go ties with people you are not comfortable with.